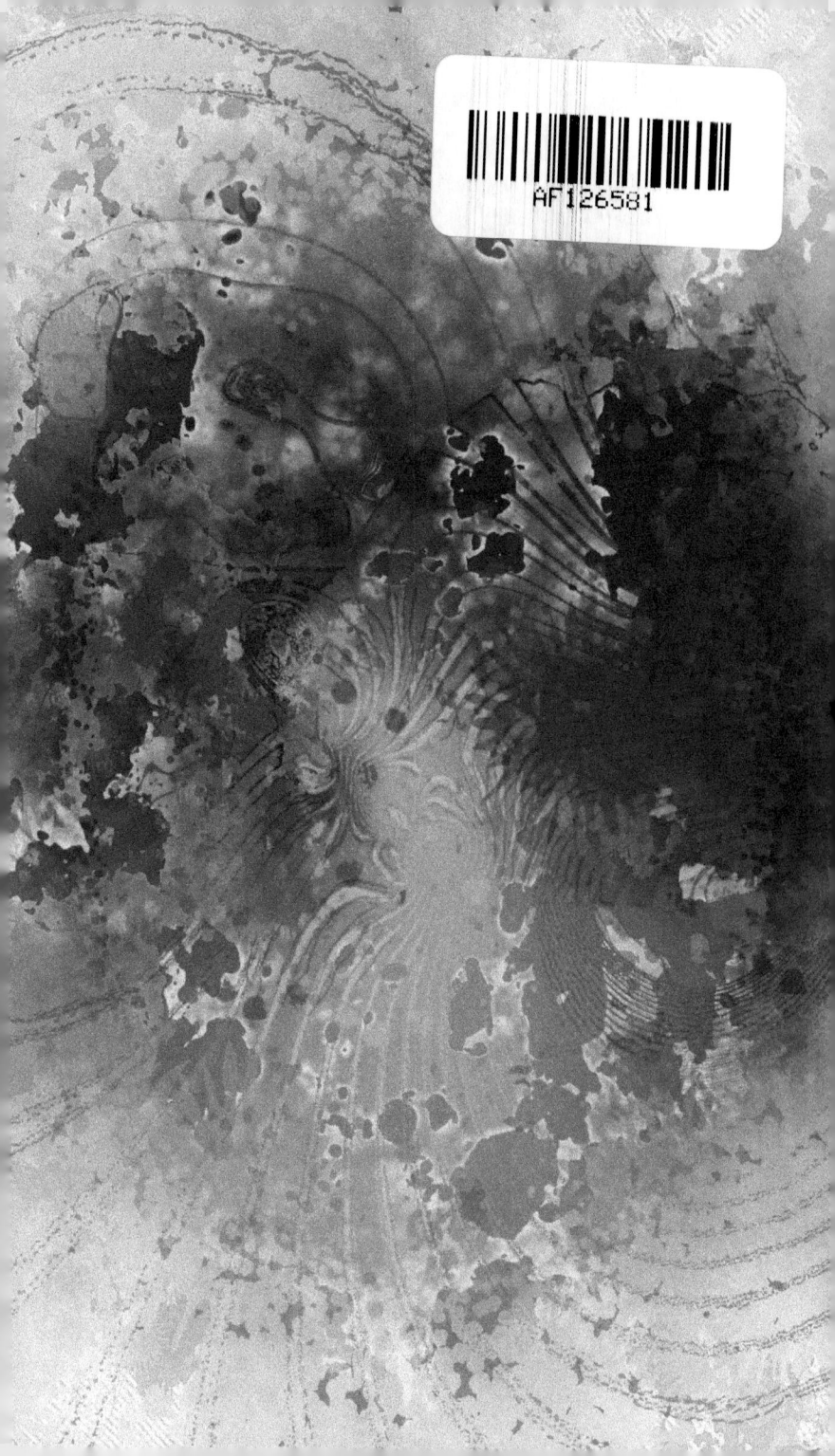

HIM OR HER OR WHATEVER

HIM OR HER OR WHATEVER

POEMS

TYLER FRIEND

Alternating Current Press
Boulder, Colorado

Him or Her or Whatever
Tyler Friend
©2022 Alternating Current Press

All material in *Him or Her or Whatever* is the property of its respective creator and may not be used or reprinted in any manner without express permission from the author or publisher, except for the quotation of short passages used inside of an article, criticism, or review. Printed in the United States of America. All rights reserved. All material in *Him or Her or Whatever* is printed with permission.

Alternating Current
Boulder, Colorado
altcurrentpress.com

ISBN: 978-1-946580-33-7
First Edition: March 2022

TABLE OF CONTENTS

They 11

I

First [comma] 17
Ass and Ra 19
Moon Fuck 20
Tree Fuck 21
Poetry Workshop or Orgy [question mark] 22
Sometimes After 23
His Ex & Tea 24
Yankee Spirits 25
Poem for a Chattanooga Night Club 26
Shit Talkin' 27
Some New Ways of Making Love 28
Try 29
Nursery Log 30
Snow 32
Poem for Charlie O's, World Famous 33
This 34
Eater 35

II

Her, the Way 41
Acorn Heart 42
Artemis Speaks of Onions & Bread 43
Titties 44
The Elms 46
Even We 47
Hell & 48
A Woman Leaves Vermont [comma] the World 49

Youphoria 50
On a Honeyed Moon 51
Sea-Stir 52
Directions to Here 54
U y l 59
U 64

III

Whatever 69
Poem for the Gaylord Opryland Hotel, Christmas Eve 70
Bi Now 74
Orchid Bae 75
Moon Heart 76
Her Tea 77
Venus Androgyne 78
Hunty 79
I, Zeus 80
Suggestions for Tinder Experiments We Could
    Conduct Together 82
Ode to the Bite 83
Weird Trans Kid 86

MATTER

About the Author 93
Author Acknowledgments 94
Colophon 96

They

Yes, I contain myself, multitudinous
& mountainous. I can be hard to navigate.

I can take your breath away. I am rock & snow
& I am melting. My heart, pudding. I contain

myself when the teacher next door says *his
or her*, when the librarian says *his or her*, when

I get *mister* & *ma'am*. I contain. I am
a container. Let me hold you. Call me

icebox, call me Tupperware. Give me your leftovers, your lasagna.
Let's laze and look at the gnats breezing. My thighs

rub like crickets. My wrists: strong, knees: weak. A week's worth
of hair on my legs, my legs with their *long*, their small ankles &
    big feet.

My proportions don't make sense to me, my belly
now big, making my breasts look even smaller.

I contain continents, have a certain countenance you can't quite
    discern. Un-
easy, is what I am most of the time.

I contain so many pronouns & you've got no idea what to do
    with them.
Figure out the sentence structure. Diagram me, would you please?

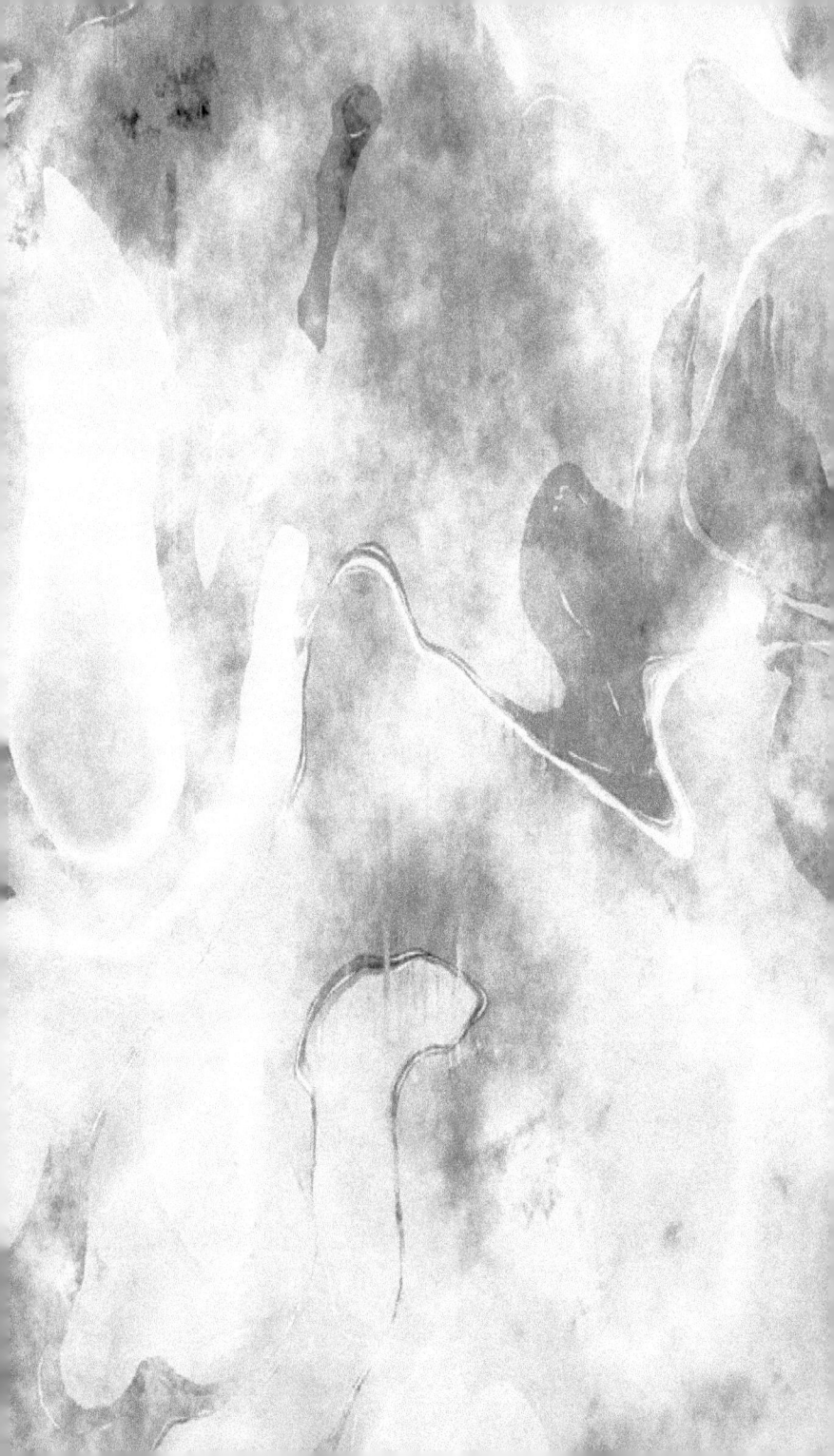

I

He's got pretty persuasion.

—R.E.M.

First [comma]

The first time a girl kissed me—
I wanted to write, *the first time
I kissed a girl*; I had already
written, *the first time a boy
kissed me*. The first time
a girl kissed me, we were

in my family's living room,
on the new couch (not the one
Ryan Buckner threw up on). Later,
we made out through the entirety
of *Snow Dogs*, into the morning, while my siblings
slept in the same room. The first time

a boy kissed me—
I should say *man*; we

were both about twenty—we
were drunk and he'd already decided
he was going home with Jake. It was a pity kiss,
really, and far too quick, on the way
to the bathroom, in the art department
of our little Catholic college.

The first time I kiss you—I wonder
if I'll ever kiss you; I wonder
if you'll ever kiss me, I should say—I'll be
in a state of wonderment. We
might be dancing; we make
such pretty things. We might be

watching an old Olsen twins movie or listening
to the Thompson Twins on cassette because we both know

the truth of tape. You might tie me up
with tape, later. Are you into that? I think
you might be; I think it might be
empowering for you, but when did all this get so
intellectualized? Is there a way for instinct and intellect
to coexist? I love your brain,

but what does your body want? I love your words
when you write them.

Is resistance to polyamory a learned behavior?
Is monogamy a preexisting condition? A way
of being, not a thing to be changed? I believe every
sexual orientation occurs naturally, but I'm not sure
it's always intrinsic. If you touch me—if I love you—
my body will respond. What does it mean?

To be gay, you don't have to like taking it
in the ass. For the record, I like taking it in the ass.

Ass and Ra

after H. D.'s "Cassandra"

Oh, hi king. Hi men. O high men,
what bitter things you are. What shit, tearing at my heart.

You scar me with light, with fire, scaring me
nameless. I name me. O why do you blind me? You dart and
 parse me, but

the dark can't entangle you. You
find my soul and ruthlessly descale it, pulling

away parts of me, my whole body
one big outbreak of eczema. But see, I name me. *Me.*

Your sun god-ness can't compete with my idgaf-ness, my
you can kiss my ass, my ass—

my ass is perfect, and I know you want me
to moon you, little sun godling, but you don't deserve it. O

I wanna make a rhyme about Ryan Gosling, but
he doesn't deserve this poem, either.

Moon Fuck

the relationship between
chemical symbol and literary symbol
is like the relationship between

fuck the moon as an expletive and
fuck the moon as in [comma] a desire to

there's a multiplicity of meanings

open your mouth
like a puckered moon
sap-stained

like a pearl popping
out of Matt Barney's bum

but nobody goes to the movies
to see people behave well

no

we want to see

the copulation & the cattle
the philosophy & the laundry
the ocean & the original sin

we want to see

Tree Fuck

Looking at you looking at your page
hands salty, steamed
broccoli on the table, able to turn you on. Broccoli
is the least sexy veggie, but
I would totally fuck a tree. I guess
I'm a size queen. Do you want
to join us? Grasp that
thick trunk, let
the bark scrape against your back, let
the leaves whisper
dirty things into
your chloroplasted veins. Surprise!

Now you're a tree and so am I. I guess
we're stuck here for a while, so we might as well
get to know each other.

Of course, there's not
a lot going on around here.

Of course,
I want
to chop you open
and give you
another ring.

Of course,
you look sexy
lying on your side,
and of course I'll yell *tim*
if you yell *ber*—but look!

There's a bear, and Tim is riding it,
and wouldn't he make such a darling lumberjack?

Poetry Workshop or Orgy [question mark]

It's usually best to start and end with a compliment.

There are different philosophies about the order in which things should happen.

Sometimes beginners can be a little shy or confused about how to get started.

Sometimes a little wine can loosen everyone up.

Use of cell phones is discouraged, but one will inevitably ring.

Not everybody will end up having the same amount of time spent on their pieces.

The men in the group will expect more attention, even though their work probably isn't as impressive.

Someone will say, *He's really grown.*

Someone will reference Derrida.

It's usually best to start and end with a compliment.

Sometimes After

after H. D.'s "Sometimes and After"

Sometimes there's no guarantee. A field
full of daisies is like a Tumblr full of cocks.

It's a dream; you're a dream.

You knock me over & latch on.
Night reconstitutes us &

day stays away, all those fevered red
apple-blossom hours.

His Ex & Tea

after H. D.'s "His Ecstasy"

He was yours, but now
I mine him. He is my quarry

& his sides rise with each tremor, struggling
& wet with the green-stone-melt, scented

green & pitiable. You are a fir tree
trying to find some loam

in these fields (no longer fields). This
is no longer a place

for singing & satyrs, but still
I mine him, mix & wine him.

Yankee Spirits

An old man from Savannah
at the liquor store is unimpressed by the way Vermont thinks
it's so liberal, the way it looks down

on the South, and then I tell him I went to school in Pittsburgh
 and it's so much worse, and
he says, it's industrial, and I'm not sure what that has to do with
 anything, but
he says, y'know, the thing about folks there is

the ones who call us fags
are the same ones who're waitin' out back.

Poem for a Chattanooga Night Club

i'm sitting here at a gay bar in the south & this queen is performing
& she's dressed like a genie & her name is Glistening Goddess

& after the show she comes over to our table & thanks us for coming
& i'm sharing my hushpuppies with a girl in a short-short dress

& Goddess says they're microwaved & i shouldn't eat them
but i want to & to my left is a man on a wooden pole

or more like a column really, like structurally significant
& he's drinking a bud light, but to my right

is a blond woman with an undercut
& her boyfriend & a confederate flag tattoo

on her shoulder & there's smoke in the air
& the sign outside says no loitering by order of the police

Shit Talkin'

after H. D.'s "Sitalkas"

Thou art the length of a gherkin, less
beautiful than any cucumber.

Touch me not. I would leave you broken.

Some New Ways of Making Love

You, holding a corpse pose.
Me, carefully eating a peach,

but cracking a tooth on the pit
anyway. You, riding a bicycle

around midnight. You, not
wearing your glasses. You,

saying, *Fuck the Police*. Me,
saying, *Fuck the Patriarchy*.

Me, driving with the windows
down and the heat cranked

up. You, unhurriedly undressing
before a bath. You, hanging

your bras out to dry. You, looking
just the way you look.

Try

after H. D.'s "Triplex," a prayer

Let them not war in me. These days, saving tidy destinies and her: twining, borne with it: mending gaily. Let them not hate me. These trees, made of the luminous gray eyes of mistresses, of honey & marble, implacable white thighs: a goddess chasing the daughter of Zeus through the beautiful skies. Let me grow by your side, inside these trees dipped in purple, in attic light, rising together.

Nursery Log

An ecological facilitation,
a slowly decaying

seedbed, sweetly
temperate: sexless reproduction.

Moths and smoke,
a humming like the mind

of a fish from empty
skies: bees—well, a bee

bearing rootbeer-colored
pollen. Potato-chip leaves

hugging other leaves: crunchy.
The wild sensitive-plant folds

when touched. It's
so cute I want to kick it.

The familiar nest-smell
of you, smeared

with a little honey
heredity. Ethnobotany:

the harmony and direction
of the fondue coast,

of sun on skin on
uneven soil. Black

tea and green tin,
granite. Kudzu helps with

headaches and induces
sweating; skunk cabbage

can cure cramps, coughs, and
convulsions: things like desire, snow.

Snow

I crossed unsalted southern roads, avoiding a Jeep dreidel, praying later on a little yellow Beetle up in Pennsylvania. A hotel room paid for by her boss: BOTA boxed: warmed by wine and exothermic energy. I wore borrowed lace and read: *Every time it starts to snow, I would like to have sex.* Synonyms for *peg*: shy, guy, test, try, nail, buttress, screw, size, nut, stud, strengthen, heave, thrust, pitch, button down, make fast, peculiarize. We looked at toe-pincher caskets and cat urns online. She told me she loved me for the second time: no take-backs now.

Poem for Charlie O's, World Famous

I have a vodka cran, & you'll order
a rum & coke, or maybe a whiskey sour.

What's the word for the bit of arm
between your elbow and your shoulder?

I don't know, but I like your *those*, & I want
to sit in the near-dark next to you, feeling

the slight pressure where our *those* are touching. This.
This is what I'm trying to talk about: the ability to remain

so fully present inside a silly hunk of meat, & not
try to race my way out of it. This. This is what I'm learning.

This

after H. D.'s "Thetis"

I

On the pavement, you
all amber & onyx, flecked

with violet & white. We
mingle in the light, slowly becoming

seaglass & gay, crimson lilies.

II

We pass
on this island

(we myrtle wood
& silt cave, we

slow stretch of beach
& chicory, chiseled moon)

when the sun slips
through us, we sing like amber.

Eater

after H. D.'s "Demeter"

I

Men throw fits,
step on temples. Smash bricks

onto foreheads or foreskins. Little
lintels, these white altars: slaughter

& burn. Meet me deep in this mystery. Mind
these tense thighs, taught & ready. I

will teach you: your
heavy gold & solid back,

marble seat. These will not help you. Stay
out of my way. I will wring you

with dragon fire & poppy juice. I have what you want—
slender waist & slight breast, many fashions. Kneel

at my plinth & I may smile down
upon you. You're caught &

you flatter me, praise & begift me. But
this is useless & I will not let you stay. I have this shell, my home

& it's fashioned just for me. No men!
Though I will bend you like Zeus, I am *woman*

& goddess & queen. I will melt you
& leave.

II

Don't ask me to go for a stroll. I ain't do that
gay shit. You're parched &

I'm the prophecy. There's precedent
for this. Take

my tablet & I will mark you
mine. My marble surface:

mystic. You're in a trance, see? Get stoned
& sleep next to me, see

forearm & phallus & foremost, this precipice.
I will push you over. You are soft, an inner thigh. You

are myrtle & crocus, entwined. All this bark
we stripped together.

III

Brace against me. I will take & break
like lightning—me! a womanly Zeus!—

enough. I'm just playing. I'm really
like a child. I am soft & full of love, a little

loaf of bread. Ivy,
slowly climbing. Knot on

an oak, resinous. I resonate. I will heal
these hearts of men, one day.

II

She's got pretty persuasion.

—R.E.M.

Her, the Way

after H. D.'s "Hermes of the Ways"

She is hard & she breaks me. I
am clear like rain & she

remakes me into wine. We play
with the wind, the wide shore.

Her waves break over me
(break me). I am a pile of salt:

little, ridged
dissolving & dubious.

Acorn Heart

after H. D.'s "Acon," after Johannes Baptista Amaltheus

I

Beat me to death with dictation.
Let me steep, then slop me everywhere.

I choose to pray to you: a dittany, a lit
litany of cypress, a frail flower.
Bud & myrrh—
all-healing herbs
folding into
flowers, hidden
in skin-thick pages. Close-
pressed. Your skin,
a page written upon. You paint
with your breath, your wanting
broken sobs, you. You, Goddess, I
will roast upon your spit.

II

Dryads drying on the shore, haunting
the groves, hanging out
with nereids in
their wet caves, all whitish & olive,
branching & risen. These ivy wreaths &
their swollen berries: altars bearing
ripe fruits, an arcade of ass & wine.

We'll shatter your fever.

The light falls, flowerlike—
hyacinths, hidden
in their valleys, burn.

Bring gifts, throw fits: Phoenician stuff, off-
erings of irises & pills & frail-headed poppies.

Artemis Speaks of Onions & Bread

after H.D.'s "Orion Dead"

These trees lift me up
& unburrow, the roots

splayed & sexy
like so many legs. Y'all think

I'm so chaste, but you just don't know
what turns me on. So I rise

when I pierce the flesh
of a wild deer &

I am not afraid to touch
the blue- & gold-veined hyacinths.

I tear up at the sight of the full flowers
& their little heads, the bulbs. I will strip

every ivory layer & lie in the black earth. I'll bend
for the ash tree & alight.

Titties

after H. D.'s "Cities"

Can you even believe? My heart, don't
waste this. We're all in the streets

& they're disgusted. No grace, no lace. Crowded
into a single house, so scared

of us, but we just play a little different. That's all. Ironic,
really, how easy it is to make them blush. We

are beautiful & take
up just enough space. We

arch perfectly, bending to our angles. We are
porchlight angels & hyacinth shadows—

black. Pavement. Fashioned out of marble.
Our titties upset them, that they can't

grasp our beauty, that we won't
let them unpack our honey. They want

to measure us. We are unrivaled. We've got
the girth & we grow fast. Our honey

seethes. O stray pollen & old dust. O men, you
once held light. What happened? You squirm

like larvae & spread. You're useless. You can't have
our honey & flowers. You are nothing

but ghosts.

The Elms

after H. D.'s "The Helmsman"

O be *we*—
always *we*, we red wind
and salt marsh. *We*—
we wood-flowers, we
wood-grass. We pine-hills and
we bramble-fruit hair: we
as buried roots and acorn-cups. We—
we green from green, we thickets,
we ankles and earth, us—
the feel of *between*, we. We tree-resin, sweat
sweet to the taste. We enchanted
tufts of love, we.

Even We

after H. D.'s "Evening"

We pass light
back & forth, from ridge

to ridge & flower to
flower. We ourselves

flower, become. We grow
faint, reach inward, blue

& lost, our hearts—
blue. Our buds are still

& shadowed. We
root, leaving leaves

& turning away from
the glass, at last.

Hell &

after H. D.'s "Helen"

All this grease, these stained hands. Still eyes
like olives & stands of white hands

reaching up. All these Grecian revels, these smiling faces.
Remember the past? That was sick. We were sick &

our daughter unborn, thank God.

A Woman Leaves Vermont [comma] the World

& we feel it. We feel it
in Tennessee, Alabama, Alaska. We feel it

in Bellingham & Way-South Texas. We feel it
in Iowa and Albuquerque, maybe most of all. I hardly knew her,

but I know what she did for us, that she cut limes for my Corona,
cooked me tacos, let me play her videogames. Was radical, wanted

to perform abortions on every street corner. Bring your own
    hanger, five dollars.
Walked with me in the middle of the street, with boxes

of wine, with her wife
& Magaly, & never once did she let anyone see her scared.

I'm scared. The first time I met my coworker at the library
she told me that her friend is trans

& that he tried to commit suicide
last month. I'm not sure why she tells me

these things, but I'm glad she feels like she can. Sometimes
being queer in the South seems so lonely, so

quiet. Sometimes it feels like we're glass floats, & sometimes
it feels like we're mastheads, & sometimes we're just humans,
    treading water.

Youphoria

You were soaked in sugar water when you were a baby, sprinkled with cinnamon. Now you're starting to ferment, ephemeral. You.

You've created yourself, a little ocean. You wash your hair on Wednesdays
and Saturdays. You beat me up with your mouth: my favorite bruise, my favorite hue.

You're the Mario Kart queen, cheesecake-sweet cheeks, cozy lips, biting hips:
wine-drinking fiend, a menthol-free Stefani dream, a lavender lover.

You think my crazy is cute, call me a kiwi, like the bird, like
no longer an ugly duckling, like transformed, don't

mention the scars, just kiss them. Your kisses
are gonna give me cavities. You're just too damn sweet.

Your lips are warm, like a fish tank. Like an aquarium. Yum. You tell me I'm beautiful and I manage to say, *Thank you*. You say, *Thank you*

for saying thank you. We're both very thankful here, thank you very much.

On a Honeyed Moon

The pan | or | ama: a crea | my cottage, nesting between honeysuckle and beebalm: | aromatic (not aromantic): a romantic land | scape, rosy. Brick floors atop small-town soil | unsoiled | and antique windows: sepia, a seeping glow, sneaking around ivy. Alabaster bedding and raspberry | rusting: serene, serendipito | us. O | pen shutters and unlocked doors, love shudders. Macro: softening already s | oft folds: a botanical belly, borderless. Thick thighs and growing fo | rests: mountaino | us and contrapposto, mar | bled, mirrored in crying eyes. Low light | push-processed. Cat | hedrals, caverno | us yawns, braids, and high- | waist shorts, film canister | s in breast pockets. Mode | led, molded: cut legs (igno | red, kissed) and thigh-highs. Becoming a candle, crad | led, red, and lit. Weeded and wined (wound) ((round)), out of focus. Developing | in darkened dorm room close | ts (pretty gay). Fair | y-pink flower hats, held | to | get | her with bobby pins, paired (syr | uped, peared), for | aged from the yard. Wine-fil | led teacups floating in the bathtub, songs about crying in grocery stores, slo | wed, steeping dark choco | late heart rot, budding: harmonio | us, trans | lucent.

Sea-Stir

after H. D.'s "Circe"

I was easy enough
to bend, over

her altar. Easy enough
to touch & be touched. I drifted

on the great sea of drink, this sea
of white ash & rock & tamarisk.

It's a risk, this. Come
& blacken my innermost forest.

Your fragrance, fragmented. All this
sea-magic. Nautical. I'm

nautilus-like, an easy
enough thing to be, I think. They cried

at the sight of my face & I prayed
only for your touch. My entreaty: *please*

come for me & (whispered): *stay*.
I pant for you & become

a sea-sound, a sea-stone. Sea
lion barking at your heels. I,

swirl of sand in the wind. I
am resonating with your frequency.

[What is your frequency, Kenny?]

It is easy enough to call men dirt
& still

summon them to my feet.
They circle me like panthers, sleek

hounds. I could let them cover my sea-caves
with ivory & onyx. Me & my rock-

fringe coral, the palace
of this whole religion.

Directions to Here

Ride on birdseed-fed bears
and bees' knees over overgrown

dirt bike paths, through ferned forests with
bruised bottles, through holes in ginkgo

leaves, in shadows, through
Spanish-tiled sewers, past

already-burnt wood: dark
and shiny. Read the off-trail

Braille. Look into the eyes
of birch trees. Share

your honey with me
and float away lazily.

Ride on midlife crisis bicycles
and imaginary friends, over the years

and through inherited memory, through
sage stillness and layers of rust dust.

Share your sports bras, wrap yourselves
up on shipping pallets: a valet ballet, like

a tumbleweed gone to sea, like
loose tongues panting: wind,

lipid soluble molecules jeopardizing
the food placed on death's metal plates.

Macerate yourself
in honey, purr your mind

into incoherent sounds:
fresh and fermented,

moonshine and slant rhyme.
Place candles, cut carnations

and unnecessary body parts, pour
in women's waters and bees' waters.

You'll need a guacamole philosophy
and lavender lemonade: twin time

sweet tea sunshine,
Cheerwine, and *we're fine*.

Radicalism is sexy. We're not
mathematicians here.

Ride on little apricot lambs
through new mountains

with stuffy noses. Search for something
resembling flannel in red,

red dirt. It's been there
since before the invention of *orange*.

I think that's where you got your hair,
that yellow scarf, those stinging eyes also

red and rotting. How can
decomposition be so dry?

Hold your little throat, your eager
calves. Look at the mountains.

Just look at them.
They are so beautiful.

Even the Sphinx is
just a pile of rocks

sometimes. Maybe staying stationary
is what makes you into a monument.

Allow yourself to be
stupidly in love

with the world. Listen
to shrunken heads and

Talking Heads. Let her hug
your face and breathe

in too much of her. Hear
the word *apricot* and die

a little bit, just a little bit more
than you usually die in a matter of

moments. Go to the bar and don't
break up with anyone, listen

to gloriously mediocre bluegrass
and poke plump seams.

Get lost in forest-full hair,
panties stained blue from new jeans

and friction. Feed the bees your
sweat and secretions and swallow

another stone. Yeah,
we're making progress.

Exchange heart-shaped stones
and trust that your secret

will be safe. It'll be safe
with me. With me,

a heart-shaped stone
is never just a stone

and nothing is exactly like
it really is. I'm sure

I saw you smirk
during the ceremony, but

that's okay, too. Ceremony
always feels a little silly.

Notice the similarity
between *Volvo* and *vulva*.

Get in. Tell me about eating hearts
and the size of rats and anything else

you can think of
to get me

to vomit up
some silly, smug

words like: *I like you*,
except you don't.

Forget about Fight Club;
let's form a Cry Club, hold

each other in one big, jerking
catharsis in the back of a minivan,

in the middle of a thunderstorm,
at the drive-in; Casper's playing.

If poems need
an argument,

my argument is that
I love you.

Uyl

after H. D.'s "Eurydice"

I

U sing me back, U
walking with lithe souls
through the hearth. I
sleep, live, flower: outlast

your arousal
& your toothlessness. I
am flying back to where lichen

drops, dead:

cinders & ash & you
& your arrogance. I am breaking, at last.
I live (unconsciously), almost
forget who I am.

Let me wait with this weight
& grow listlessly, peacefully:
resting within resin, dining
on the forgotten past.

II
Hear the flame & the flame,
the black & the red
sneaking dark & light, growing
colorless. You turn me, reinhabiting my shell:
we're sleeping in. You turn my back
to lace. Make haste, don't hesitate. Just bend your face
down to me, aflame (red) & wanting, waiting. Your light
crosses my face, glancing off. What is it that you saw?

Earth & hyacinth, a fissure forming
in the rock where you struck. The azure assures
us, the crocuses & lightning veins of white, swift
& running down my thighs.

III
Safe from the fringes, bending
over the edge of bed, the edge
of earth, all the flowers cut

& are cut & are
lost; everything is lost.

IV
Crocuses croaking, callused, walled
off & blue, lost in the depths, lost

& flowering; I could have taken them. They took me, took
my breath away. There are enough of them—more than me—
supporting me more than earth. Pass this time with me, beneath
the earth, this tree. If you catch what I'm saying, then hold it.
Turn its pages, & all those flowers pressed inside its Sapphic
    heart. Read it.

The pages tear away
so prettily.

V

So for your air
& your ruthlessness, I
have lost you. A directive: open to the
flowers, the souls of
earthiness, the passing of light. Reach
for the roof, only it's not there. You

have your own light. You
are present, preset, permanent.

Yet, I tell you this:
such loss is no loss, such terror coiling
& strands & pitfalls, blackness,
such tearing: no loss. Hell,
you're worth more
than the earth & anything above it. Hell, you're more
than the flowers & air & veins of light.

Your veins glow in my presence, they long
to be free of your skin & are also complete,

completely content. My Hell,
you are no worse than the flowers who speak with the spirits above.

VI

Against your back, I
am your favor, little splendor for you, held.
Why don't you stay? I have more light to give,

more flowers. I should tell you, I would turn
for you. I would become that

which I cannot sink into, that.

VII

I myself am flowers, my thoughts
fevered in your presence, blowing.

I light myself
& your spirit is with me.

I am small. I know this. Hell must break me
before I am yours. I am a red rose

& the dead pass between us.

U

You're in the mirror, in your panties, saying

>HEY GURL, DID U KNOW I LIKE U

What does LIKE U mean in this context?

>a) APPRECIATE UR FRIENDSHIP
>b) WANNA HAVE SEX WITH U
>c) AM IN LOVE WITH U
>d) All of the above

It's seven degrees in Vermont, and now
I know that. And now I know you remember

touching my thigh at that party, the one
where we threw grapes into each other's pretty mouths.

I'm trying to revise my vision
of you, but mimesis is boring, isn't it? Isn't it

so silly to think of you as art?
As art, you're probably a failure. Aren't we all?

All of us are too beautiful
and too ugly to be art, all

at the same time. At the same time,
isn't that what love is?

III

God damn your confusion.

—R.E.M.

Whatever

Yes, my preferred pronoun is *whatever*. As in,
Whatever can do whatever whatever wants. Thank you

for guessing; you are the first
man to do so. I usually receive

he or *she*, sometimes even *they*, but
I have never felt quite so seen.

I know you
meant to be insulting, but

I was only shaking because
I was laughing

& yes, I'll renew your library card for you.

Poem for the Gaylord Opryland Hotel, Christmas Eve

Ice skating in fifty-degree weather
only helps it feel a little less
like we're in Tennessee, a little less
like there are fat men in camo
& T-shirts with slogans like
all rifles matter and
black ducks matter.

Why is camo so bad
at being inconspicuous? A little
Chinese-American boy
named Matthew
is very concerned
that the hot chocolate
is no longer hot. His dad is
his hero. Matthew thinks
his dad skates great.

We used to come here
to look at the Christmas decorations
when I was little, but I never noticed
that there are bars
every fifteen feet. You can pay
an extra ten dollars to get
your Merry Margarita in a cowboy
boot-shaped glass with mini Christmas lights.

A waitress named Amanda
misgenders me (??? she thinks),
& then is very sorry about it, very sweet,
not able to stop talking about it, says she's very ____
(accepting, open-minded, choose a synonym), that she
herself is *obviously* a woman, but that she's
very *alternative* in other ways. I know
I have it so much easier than so
many people, but I'd like
to go
one day
without having
to make someone feel better
about the way they're making me uncomfortable.

Back in the room, we watch
an animal documentary. There has been
a 3000% increase in rhinoceros poaching
just in the past three years. In Chinese medicine,
it is believed that rhino horns can cure all sorts of ailments,
but David Attenborough doesn't take it seriously.

Every black rhino in Africa is a target.

Every black rhino in America is a target. In this
stanza, *Black rhino* means *Black man*, means *brown man*, means
woman & *Jew* & *Muslim*, means queer, means
Camden who doesn't catcall on the streets of Pittsburgh, means
Robbie whose full name is Robinson, means
Liz giving pap smears at the clinic, but
there's always the hope that one day the black rhino will make it
off the endangered species list.

I choose to place my hope
in the group of women who show up
at an old-money hotel in Middle Tennessee
during Christmas, decked out in hijabs
& purple lipstick, who are fucking owning it, &

I place my hope just as equally
in the tiny old woman in the H&M, furtive
& nervous in her burka, &

I choose to place my hope
in this new generation: these straight boys in skinny jeans
& eyeliner, these statuesque goth girls &
their chubby boyfriends, &

I even choose to place my hope
in the red-necked ex-drug-addict working
at the Tex-Mex restaurant, who doesn't know
whether to call me *sir*, who thinks it's weird
that my blood orange margarita
isn't the color of blood or oranges, but who knows
enough not to ask if my partner and I want separate checks, &

I choose to place my hope
in my partner who was so proud
of herself for referring to the high schooler
at the ticket booth as *they*.

Bi Now

after H. D.'s "Birds in Snow"

See: how we race across the rumble-place: the bright heavens & screen-printed clouds, careful & candlelike: melting & mystic: a lore (alluring), a symbol outlining her eyes: a gate (agate). Her eyelids, ancient rites, a garden. Now: the gay & the very-gay: we're not just garden-variety avant-garde now, we queers are acclaimed. In the caravan, her glyphs elongate, here: here king and kinglet lay, here Prince and lady rest, mythic queens, here, unsleeping & holy, here: heretical & fair, tracing slowly.

Orchid Bae

after H. D.'s "At Baia"

In a dream, you brought me
such lovely, perilous things:

orchards of orchids, piling
high. You say, *I'll give you my blue veins,*

my unkissed throat & your hands
take me, your hands like the sea drift over my orchid head

so carefully, so full, your hands
fall & lift, gently. I am such fragile stuff.

Stuff me with your flower—ah ah, how was it
you sent me this dream, your form, your scent

heavy and perilous—perilous!—orchids piled, playing,
a folded sheet underneath, rolling around in your words.

Moon Heart

The katydids are all saying
Katie did Katie did Katie did

only they won't tell me what you did
and the damselflies love

their damn selfies, and so do I!
because I love

when you lean over
in front of my face

and I can feel
your breath on my skin, creating

a thin layer of atoms
that were once inside of you.

Her Tea

after H. D.'s "Heat"

The wind lends me heat,
tatters me. Drops

fruit into thigh-high thickets. She
presses pears into me, blunts

me. I rain & I blotch, having
visions of decapitated pigeons &

peering through grass. She cuts it, turns it
into a path.

Venus Androgyne

Come eat—circumvent black fur, tent
of femme, little shelter. Promenade and purl.

When the vial emerges, bend and greet it—
thank it for what it gives me. Imagine it

glass, classy, little phallic chandelier. Imagine it
videogame medpack, giver of hearts. Imagine it

coffee and wine and ice-cream. Imagine it
the leaves of a Japanese maple, just beginning

to turn. Imagine it whiteout, used
on all the parts of me that say *man*, like one

of Mary's erasures, leave only the *wo*.

Hunty

after H. D.'s "Huntress"

Come & blunt me. Grind
& roll me. Don't spare me,

spear me. My chest is already beaten.
You're so hot & you bear me. Lead me

in this chase. I am not chaste, no Art-
emis. We wind down hills, through

the hot froth of bogs, clods
stuck on jeans.

I am parched, and you
are the wineskin.

I, Zeus

after H. D.'s "Let Zeus"

I

I'm not done with this, these
inanimates, but you can come

with. Chill.

I don't tolerate loneliness well, but
your loveliness keeps me awake. I obdurate

bitterness & you're a lemon. Squeeze into
that stream & I'll fuck you on her banks. You

on your knees, on this frigid night. It's down-
right evil. Let's do it

in the Parthenon, your splendor
on display. Keep your fear at bay, face down

in the inviolate dawn.

II

Men can marry you, but women—
we can break you. It's innate, this

strength. We'll strike down the plutocracy
& vacation on Pluto. Pardon me, this

ego. You'll outlive me, but
that's deliberate.

III

You wear my dress & all
the men gaze at you. Your body

is obstinate & it turns me to clay. I can't stand
it. Intolerable desire & all that.

IV

When you scar me, I want
to wear your ring. These Georgians

don't understand. I feel meager
in your storm. I am blown

by you. Fashion me into a bird, something
with wings.

V

Myrrh-flower & all
these men. I have them.

I spread them, again
& again.

Suggestions for Tinder Experiments We Could Conduct Together

    1.
Let's roleplay—you be the boy, I'll be
the girl. We can see how long it takes you to send me a dick pic.

    2.
Let's catfish straight boys, pretending
we're a Sapphic couple looking for a third to join us.

    3.
Let's create fake accounts and try
to seduce each other.

    4.
Let's see how long I can convince the country boys
that I'm a cis woman, nudes included.

    5.
Let's exchange nudes and see
if we can keep it platonic.

    6.
Let's make Mike an account and only make him visible
to men, see what happens.

    7.
Let's change our profile pics
and get so drunk we forget who we are.

Ode to the Bite

When you put your teeth
on me, on my shoulder, my knee—

when you put your lips
on me, my cheek, the top of my head—

when you put your lipstick
on me, my lips, not at all involved

with your lips, except
through this color, I wonder

at the way the stars rest, the way my brain
stops skipping steps, stops

working so goddamn hard
and never getting anything done.

*

O light bite O slight suggestion O wonder and plunder
O little purple lightning crack and soft slow thunder rumble
O little engine that could O flesh and rot and heat
O heart beat through teeth O furniture of fate O little lovely slate
O fairytale kink O
mouth blink O flounder and sink, ink in the sink
O night O light O little, intimate fight
O survival O revival of ancient rites
O vampire O blood O goddamn O, I never thought
it would feel this much. I mean, I know
you're literally getting under my skin, getting
inside me, but what is this *me*
I'm talking about now? Is it possible
for anyone to literally get inside me, or
is the *me* I'm talking about really just my body?
What if *me* is not my body? Or, worse, what if it is?

How am I supposed to like myself if
me equals body,
        equals man,
                equals dick,
                       equals something
I will never like (on myself)—yours is fine. Yours
could be inside me, too, if you want—like your teeth, like
    your soul   —   your soul
can cuddle with mine if she wants.

   *

Have you ever bitten anyone?
Neither have I, but I hear

it's like purple taffy, like cartwheeling
down the boardwalk

with an oversized ice cream cone, like
wading in the shallows, like consuming

heart-shaped cake. Or hurt cake. What happens
when consumption leads to pain

leads to pleasure. Purple seems like the color
of a bite. Like, if I had to assign *bite* a color,

it would definitely be purple. Biting
is the ultimate form of closeness and conclusion

because it can lead to digestion
and so many other things.

Weird Trans Kid

Weird Trans Kid's bladder is the size of a squirrel—
not a squirrel's bladder, but an actual squirrel, a chubby gray one.
Weird Trans Kid doesn't know which restroom to use. Is tired
of all mainstream trans politics revolving around restrooms.
Thinks restrooms are improperly named. Wants to rename
them anxietyrooms. Wants to rename them imnotsurehowthese
    placesareapatriarchalconstructionbutimsuretheyare.
Doesn't know whether to wrap the towel around his waist or
    his tits, too. Gets turned on
by cold showers and full moons and long car rides. Probably
has a small dick. Or a really large clitoris.
Or no genitals at all. Who knows?
Probably looks like a Barbie doll down there.
In any case, they probably don't get laid very often. Fetishized plenty,
though. Weird Trans Kid has plenty of kinks herself, likes to call
her girlfriend Ma'am and Mama. Probably because Weird Trans Kid
never got to be a little girl for real. For real, though,
Weird Trans Kid really is pretty weird, even
without the Trans part. I guess we should talk
about the Kid part, too—Kid's not really a kid anymore.
Kid's twenty-five. Kid just doesn't know
how to colloquially describe an adult in gender-neutral terms.
Kid grew up calling all their friends' parents Mr. [First Name],
    Ms. [First Name]. Would it surprise you
to learn that Kid played baseball for fifteen seasons, made it
to the all-stars, danced the cha cha slide? Had two parents,
two siblings, two dogs? The dogs are the selling point here.
That's what you're supposed to relate to.
People LOVE dogs. Unless they're cat people.
Nobody seems to love both cats and dogs, at least not equally.
I'm stuck in traffic in Kentucky, or maybe Ohio.
There's a car in front of me with a bumper sticker
that reads PROMOTE DIVERSITY and it has little illustrations
of different dog breeds. If I were a dog, everyone would love me.
Or perhaps a goat.

ABOUT THE AUTHOR

TYLER FRIEND is a poet and designer who was grown (and is still growing) in Tennessee. Their poetry has appeared in *Tin House*, *Hobart*, *Hunger Mountain*, and elsewhere. Tyler's chapbook *Bunker* is available in Third Man Books' Literarium vending machine, in the London store. This is their first full-length collection.

AUTHOR ACKNOWLEDGMENTS

Many thanks, firstly, to my mom, my brother, and my sister for putting up with me. This book never would have happened without them.

Thank you to my MFA cohort: Amelia, Amy, CJ, Jad, Katie, and Magaly for shaping my writing and my personhood in profound ways. They read and encouraged the first drafts of many of these poems, and "Nursery Log" steals lines from all of them.

Thank you to all of my many teachers, especially Allison Hedge Coke, Elizabeth Powell, Jensen Beach, Kendra DeColo, Mary Ruefle, Matthew Dickman, Miciah Bay Gault, Michelle Gil-Montero, Sean Prentiss, and Trinie Dalton, all of whom did important things for me at important times.

Thank you to H. D. and Michael Stipe, who have also taught me.

Thanks to Leah and Alternating Current Press for making this book into a real thing that is holdable.

The italicized line in "Snow" is from Mary Ruefle's poem of the same name.

The lines on the section dividers come from the song "Pretty Persuasion" by R.E.M.

"Her Tea" first appeared in *Ampersonate* (Choose the Sword Press).

"Bi Now" first appeared in *Queer, Rural, American*, a microanthology from *Miracle Monocle*.

I'm very grateful to the following journals, who first gave these poems a home, often in earlier forms and sometimes under different names: *Atlanta Review, Cleaning Up Glitter, Deluge, Drunk in a Midnight Choir, Generation, Glass: A Journal of Poetry, Hawaii Review, Hobart, Hunger Mountain, The Journal of Compressed Creative Arts, Love's Executive Order, Mud Season Review, NILVX, Pamplemousse, Paper Darts, peculiar, Poetry South, Q/A, Rag Queen Periodical, Screen Door Review, Spilled Milk Magazine, Tin House, VIDA Review,* and *Yes Poetry*.

Lastly, shoutout to all the folks I haven't already mentioned who appear in these poems: my exes and crushes, my childhood friends, the kids who hung out in the art room, a not-insignificant portion of the Greek pantheon, the man who worked at the liquor store in Montpelier, grumpy old library patrons, Tim, Mike, Brianna, Ellen, David Attenborough, Glistening Goddess, N.W.A., Mary-Kate and Ashley Olsen, the Thompson Twins, the Talking Heads, Matthew Barney, Gwen Stefani, Ryan Gosling, and Jacques Derrida.

COLOPHON

The edition you are holding is the First Edition of this publication.

The titles are set in Din, created by Albert-Jan Pool at Foundry. The Alternating Current Press logo is set in Portmanteau, created by JLH Fonts. All other text is set in Athelas, created by Veronika Burian and José Scaglione. All fonts used with permission; all rights reserved.

Cover designed by Leah Angstman, with images by Moose Photos. The Alternating Current lightbulb logo created by Leah Angstman, ©2013, 2022 Alternating Current. Interior artwork by Gerd Altmann, Steve Johnson, Prawny, Kseniya Lapteva, Allen Henderson, and Astoko. All images used with permission; all rights reserved.

Other Works from
Alternating Current Press

All of these books (and more) are available at
Alternating Current's website: altcurrentpress.com.

altcurrentpress.com

Printed in the USA
CPSIA information can be obtained
at www.ICGtesting.com
LVHW070810190923
758612LV00004B/490